Bitcoin

The Ultimate Beginner's Guide to Understanding Bitcoin

(Learn How to Mine, Trade and Invest in Bitcoin and Earn Serious Money)

Table of Contents

Introduction 4

Chapter 1: Understanding Bitcoin 7
Where Did the Concept Come From? 7
What Is a Bitcoin? 9
Why Does Bitcoin Exist? 11
What Are the Alternatives? 14

Chapter 2: How Bitcoin Works 17
How Does Bitcoin Compare to Traditional Currencies? 17
How Are Bitcoins Acquired, Traded, and Used? ... 21

Chapter 3: Buying Bitcoin 24
Understanding Cryptocurrency Exchanges 26
Choosing the Best Exchange for Your Needs 28
    Where Are You Located? 29
    What Method of Payment Will You Use? 30
    What Are the Fees? 30
    Do They Deal with Bitcoin? 33
    Is It Credible? 34
The Buying Process 35
    Choose Your Exchange 36
    Buy Bitcoins from the Exchange 36
    Transfer Bitcoins to a Wallet 37
    Store or Spend Bitcoins 38

Chapter 4: Storing Bitcoin 39
Types of Bitcoin Wallets 39
Understanding and Using Hot Wallets 41
Understanding and Using Cold Wallets 44

Chapter 5: Trading Bitcoin 51
Returning to the Cryptocurrency Exchange.......... 52
What to Trade, What to Keep 53
When to Pull the Trigger....................................... 56

Chapter 6: Mining Bitcoin 60
What Is Mining?... 60
How Does Mining Work?....................................... 62
Is Mining Still Profitable?..................................... 65
Understanding Mining Pools................................ 68
Conclusion on Mining.. 71

Chapter 7: The Future of Bitcoin 73
Is It Here to Stay? 74
Will It Always Be Bitcoin? 76
   Faster, Cost-Effective Bank Transfers............... 80
   Increase in Global Remittances......................... 81
   Safe Money for Developing Countries............... 82
   Increased E-Commerce Benefits 84
   Empowers the Public 85

Conclusion 87

Introduction

Cryptocurrencies have been a hot topic lately, and not just in the financial industry. In fact, they're no longer restricted to the professional world at all! At one time, the only two groups of people who were heavily invested in cryptocurrencies were those in the financial industry and computer scientists who were actively watching and involved with the creation of cryptocurrencies. Nowadays, they have become a household topic. Everyone is interested in getting started with investing in these currencies and for good reason. While no one knows exactly what they are capable of yet, everyone knows that they are here to stay.

All of this cryptocurrency development started with one single cryptocurrency: Bitcoin. Bitcoin was the pioneer of modern cryptocurrency. While there were other attempts beforehand, this was the first of its kind to become successful. As a result, it has remained the most popular and continued to top the charts in regards to value and growth. People everywhere want to get started with investing in Bitcoin to earn their share of profits, especially after all of the media and press attention on people becoming overnight millionaires as a result of this fascinating new currency.

In fact, since you are reading this, I can bet that *you* are also interested in how you can get started with Bitcoin! This guide was created to help you with just that. You will learn about the pioneer of modern cryptocurrencies, how you can begin buying and trading Bitcoins, important information about how to store your investment, Bitcoin mining, and where Bitcoin is expected to go in the future. By the end of this book, you should feel confident in your knowledge surrounding this phenomenal currency and how you can get involved in it today. If you are ready to know more, let's get started!

This book was designed to explain the important things you need to know about Bitcoin. Intense effort and commitment were poured down on this book to make it accurate and to provide as much information as possible. Please enjoy reading!

Chapter 1: Understanding Bitcoin

The first useable currency of its kind, Bitcoin is a pioneer in cryptocurrency technology. Despite the introduction of numerous other forms of cryptocurrency since the launch of Bitcoin, none have held up as powerfully as Bitcoin has. Both in regards to popularity and financial strength, Bitcoin has continually proved itself and the strength it has within modern society. But what is Bitcoin exactly? Let's take a look.

Where Did the Concept Come From?

The concept of cryptocurrency came about around two or three decades ago. Back in the 1990s, computer scientists began attempting to craft a form of currency that would be entirely dealt with online. Over time, we began to see symptoms of these advancements. Debit cards, credit cards, and the entire concept of being able to store your currencies online without having to carry around physical money were all born out of the idea that gave birth to cryptocurrency itself.

Despite more than a decade of attempted cryptocurrency creations, no new forms of currency ever really "stuck". The concept was a fascinating one, but the strategies they had been using to design cryptocurrencies left many security risks. For example, should the system be hacked, large amounts of money could be filtered out and essentially stolen. Since computer technology and the concept of the internet were all so new at the time, very few people had an understanding of how any form of currency could be designed without hacking becoming an issue.

Still, computer scientists continued to try. Several different forms of cryptocurrencies were conceptualized and tested, but none of them ever held up against the security tests. That is until 2009 when a computer scientist who goes by the alias "Satoshi Nakamoto" designed Bitcoin. Bitcoin was far from being the first cryptocurrency concept ever to exist, but it *was* the first one that was actually feasible and could be used on a wide scale. So, after its introduction, Bitcoin exploded in popularity and has since evolved into a form of currency that people all around the globe are talking about, monitoring and, best of all, investing in. Bitcoin has turned many people into overnight millionaires, and it can do the same for you.

What Is a Bitcoin?

A Bitcoin is a form of cryptocurrency that is entirely based in the online space. There is no physical form of currency attached to Bitcoin. Instead, it is an encryption technique used to represent a fund. This technique is then responsible for the storing, trading, and spending of these "funds" or encryption codes.

Bitcoin itself operates in an entirely decentralized manner. This is the exact technology that made it stand up against the other cryptocurrencies and become the first successful cryptocurrency the world has ever seen. The decentralized system means that Bitcoin relies on a series of "nodes" or systems that are responsible for "hashing" the movement of the coins themselves. All nodes must be in agreeance with one another to accept a trade or transaction. This technology is what overcame the many security concerns of previously attempted cryptocurrencies. It also gave birth to an incredible new form of technology known as "blockchain", which is another topic for another time.

Aside from the technical jargon, a Bitcoin is essentially a form of currency. While it is not recognized or owned by any governing body, Bitcoin is widely recognized as a legitimate form of currency that can be used in place of traditional currencies. As they continue to grow in popularity, more and more companies are accepting them as a form of payment in exchange for products or services.

This currency is unlike any other in that, since

there is no governing body, it is not restricted to a particular region. Bitcoins can be spent and traded across borders and nations without any need to worry about banks, currency exchanges or other disruptions that can result in expensive fees and timely transactions. This is a global currency that anyone can access, use, and trade, regardless of where you are stationed.

Why Does Bitcoin Exist?

Bitcoin exists for a number of reasons. Primarily, it is believed that Bitcoin was more of an experiment used to test the boundaries and capabilities of computers and global technology that is based on the internet. However, there are many additional reasons as to why Bitcoin continues to exist and what people are doing with it.

Bitcoin would not continue to exist if people were not interested in it and all that it is capable of. In the earlier days of Bitcoin, there were many darker uses for it. Because it was the only form of currency that could be used in completely anonymous transactions across borders, it was viewed as a means to trade and sell illegal goods without repercussions. While this type of activity likely still exists, it has shrunken considerably in size. Since many governing bodies have come together to shut down these forms of activities and the currency itself has grown in awareness and understanding, the majority of users are now using the cryptocurrency for positive and genuine reasons.

Now that it has found its place in society and has become used for genuine intentions that are outside of illegal activity and gain, many average people are becoming fascinated by the technology and the capabilities it has. Bitcoin enables people to invest in a currency that appears to have an ever-expanding price tag, as well as invest in all that this currency represents and the many positive benefits it may have on society in the future.

Bitcoin is now an opportunity for people to easily send money across borders without paying enormous fees or otherwise losing their money to bank charges. This is wonderful for those with families that live elsewhere in the world as they can seamlessly send funds without having to pay astronomical fees for these funds. Also, traditional currencies can rise and drop in value rapidly, so being able to send in real time means that you do not run the risk of the exchange rate devaluing in the several days it takes for an overseas transaction to be completed.

Another reason why Bitcoin is likely rising in popularity is due to the newness of it. Many are excited to see where this goes and are eager to explore a world whereby a currency is upgraded and digitized. The many opportunities that become available through the use of a currency such as Bitcoin are enough to excite many, and therefore people are eager to get on board and begin to show their support early on. In addition, by investing now, you give yourself the potential to significantly increase the value of your net worth. It is never too soon to get involved!

What Are the Alternatives?

Since you are learning about the investment values of Bitcoin, I feel it is important that you also understand the alternatives that are available. Please note that these alternatives are being written at the time of this publication, and therefore the information may change and evolve over time. It is important that you conduct your own research at the time of your investment to ensure that you are completely educated about the investment you are about to make. It is simply proper investment etiquette.

Now, before you begin investing in Bitcoin, it is important that you understand why it is the best cryptocurrency to invest in at this time. While there certainly are many other alternatives, none seem to be skyrocketing in popularity *or* value as rapidly as Bitcoin has. In a little less than a decade, Bitcoin has gone from being worth $0 to being worth over $10,000 USD at one point. It continues to hover up around the five-figure mark, although obviously the value fluctuates just as many other currencies do. However, in the long-term history of Bitcoin, it has clearly increased exponentially.

The alternatives to Bitcoin include coins such as Litecoin, Altcoin, Bitcoin Cash, Peercoin, Ethereum, and Namecoin. There are several others that exist, but these are regularly considered as feasible alternatives to Bitcoin. While each of these coins has their own unique aspects and values, none seem to compare when it comes to Bitcoin. Some people do prefer to diversify their portfolio by investing in the most popular alternatives—Litecoin and Ethereum—but the popularity still resides within Bitcoin. None of the other coins even compare to the incredible value of Bitcoin at this time.

It is unknown whether any of these alternatives will ever take over, but in the history and present times of cryptocurrency, Bitcoin has always topped the charts with major gaps in value. This may be because Bitcoin was the original and therefore is considered the most well-known cryptocurrency. It may also be because this is the oldest coin and therefore people see it as stabler than alternatives that are significantly younger on the market.

It is important that, while you invest in Bitcoin, you continue to monitor the success and growth of other cryptocurrencies. Again, it is simply proper investment etiquette. You want to make sure that you are always investing your funds in areas where you will get maximum gain and where you will be benefitted most. At this time, however, starting with Bitcoin is considered to be the fastest way to maximize your gains and increase your earnings through cryptocurrency. It also remains the stablest cryptocurrency around, with the most reliable rate of growth since its release.

Chapter 2: How Bitcoin Works

Now that you have an idea of what Bitcoin is, including its history and why people are so interested in it, you are likely wondering how the currency works. As you already know, it is a decentralized currency that holds value primarily because the general public *gives* it value. You also understand that it is a completely digitized form of currency that has no physical or tangible form whatsoever. Now, however, you may be wondering exactly how Bitcoin actually works. Let's take a look at how Bitcoin compares to traditional currencies and the actual process of acquiring and using Bitcoins.

How Does Bitcoin Compare to Traditional Currencies?

There are many similarities and differences between Bitcoin and traditional currencies. By now, you are likely aware of some of the most painstakingly obvious differences; for example, the decentralized system that governs Bitcoin, which is not owned, operated or controlled by any government or region. Also, Bitcoin is a coin that holds value based off of what the global population determines, based on supply and demand. Since so many people within the world are fascinated by and interested in this currency, it holds value. Alternatively, traditional currencies hold value because the government says so and the economy is determined based off of the government and corporations.

There are many other differences between Bitcoin and traditional currencies, however. So that you can understand exactly what Bitcoin is and why it is worth investing in, let's take a brief look at some of these differences and what they mean for you. These are important to understand as they directly impact the value of Bitcoin and the very reason why people are so interested in continuing to invest in these coins.

First of all, if a person has one dollar, they have one dollar. This dollar can only be owned by one person. However, based on the nature of Bitcoin, a single Bitcoin can be rationed out to a million people. This is because you have the power to buy a percentage of a Bitcoin, rather than having to buy one entire Bitcoin. This makes investing in the coin easy because you are not required to buy an entire coin for the value that typically rates up in the thousands of dollars at this point. Instead, you can buy a percentage of a coin and still gain profits based off of the increasing value of the Bitcoin itself. For example, you could purchase 10% of a coin for $100 if the coin was worth $1000. Then, if the coin inflated to a value of $10,000, your 10% would inflate to $1000. You would still have an incredible profit gain despite not owning an entire coin.

Next, Bitcoin transactions have a much higher safety value than traditional transactions. A surprisingly common form of con that happens in the traditional currency world exists when people perform a transaction based off of their debit or credit card then revoke the transaction after they have received their products or services. Essentially, they end up receiving them for free because they reversed the transaction by falsely claiming that they never received their products or services. Without any tangible proof, the company who has become a victim of this fraud cannot re-reverse the charge to get their profits back. This can result in companies losing massive amounts of income. With Bitcoin, however, once the transaction has been processed it is done. You cannot reverse the process or erase the transaction from the history of transactions. Therefore, you cannot double-spend currency. Once it is sent, it is gone. The company you have sent it to becomes responsible for sending back any refunds, should a refund be required.

Another thing to consider is that, while Bitcoin is free to use, there are some fees that you will have to pay. Still, they are considerably less than those imposed by banks. When it comes to banks, you pay a fee to the bank for using it, plus a fee for converting funds if that is required, plus a transaction fee. There can be many other fees involved too. However, if you use Bitcoin, you choose how much you want to pay to miners for your transaction to be completed. You can choose to conduct a free transaction in which case the transaction will take much longer but will cost you significantly less. Or you can choose to pay a fee to a miner and then your transaction becomes a higher priority and therefore is conducted significantly quicker. The fascinating part of this, however, is that you get to choose how much of a fee you are willing to pay. If you don't want to pay any fee, you can simply choose to take the longer and more time-consuming route and bypass the fees altogether.

How Are Bitcoins Acquired, Traded, and Used?

Bitcoins are similar in function to traditional currency. How they are acquired, however, is slightly different. With traditional currencies, we are typically paid by someone. This can come by way of being paid for your products or services or being paid through payroll or for doing work for someone. This is typically deposited straight into your bank account, and then you can use the funds for your own pleasure.

With Bitcoin, however, it is slightly different. While some companies are starting to pay their employees using Bitcoin, many do not. For that reason, you typically acquire Bitcoin by purchasing it at a cryptocurrency exchange. This is like a form of stock market that is used specifically for cryptocurrencies. You purchase your coins through the exchange, and then you store them in a form of wallet. There are two types of wallets, which you will learn about later. There are hot wallets and cold wallets. Once you are ready to sell or use your Bitcoin, you will simply ensure that they are in your hot wallet and then conduct the transaction. The transaction process itself will depend on how you intend to use the Bitcoins. If you want to sell them, you will return to the cryptocurrency exchange and sell them there. If, however, you want to use them, you simply acquire the personal key information for the person you want to send them to. Then you send them, and they leave your wallet and appear in someone else's once the transaction is complete.

Using Bitcoin is similar to using a credit card online. While there are some very clear differences between the two, the general idea is the same. Both use funds that are already digitized, and both simply require you to complete a transaction process, which takes the funds out of your account and places them in someone else's. Once you understand the logistics of the process, it becomes much easier.

Now that you understand what Bitcoins are, how they work, and how to use them, it is time to get into the good stuff! In the following chapters, we will explore how you can buy, store, sell and use, and profit from Bitcoin. You will also learn more about where people believe Bitcoin is going and what the future prognosis for this cryptocurrency is. If you are ready to get started, let's go!

Chapter 3: Buying Bitcoin

The first step to really getting involved with Bitcoin is purchasing Bitcoins themselves. After all, you can't do much if you don't have any in your possession! Before you begin purchasing Bitcoins, it is a good idea to have an understanding of how the process works. Be sure to read all the way through this book before purchasing your first coins to ensure that you are aware of how they work, how to use them, how to safely store them, and how to sell them so that you can earn a profit. Having a thorough understanding of this knowledge beforehand will assist you in making proper and educated decisions around your investment choices. After you have read through this title, you can come back to this chapter and follow it step by step to help you through the entire process in action!

Buying Bitcoin is unlike acquiring funds of any other kind. With traditional currencies, you acquire your coins by earning them. Typically, you are paid them either in exchange for products or services or as a payout of sorts. You may also receive them as a gift. You can then choose to keep your currencies local or you can exchange them through your bank to acquire an alternative type of currency. Everything is generally done through the bank.

Cryptocurrencies, such as Bitcoin, are completely different, however. You do not acquire these through your local bank. In fact, your bank has nothing to do with them. While some companies have begun paying employees in Bitcoins, this does not actually stand to be the most readily available way to acquire the cryptocurrency. At least not yet. Instead, the best thing you can do is purchase your Bitcoins through a Bitcoin exchange. In this chapter, you will learn all about Bitcoin and cryptocurrency exchanges and how you can acquire your coins through these exchanges.

Understanding Cryptocurrency Exchanges

Put very simply, a cryptocurrency exchange is somewhat like a stock market specifically for cryptocurrencies. These exchanges are available online and can be accessed through your browser. Some of the larger exchanges have even generated mobile applications that you can download, which allow you to purchase and sell your Bitcoins through there too.

On these exchanges, many different types of currencies are available. Some may deal exclusively in Bitcoins, but most have expanded to include a fairly healthy selection of cryptocurrencies that you can purchase. For the purpose of this book, we are solely going to focus on Bitcoin. While you can also take a look at other cryptocurrencies along the way, it is typically advised that you begin by investing in and mastering one cryptocurrency before expanding to diversify your portfolio.

When it comes to understanding cryptocurrency exchanges, there is really only one strong piece of information that you need to know: this is the only place you can purchase and sell your coins. Again, you may choose to accept to be paid in Bitcoin and thus acquire them in exchange for your products and services, but, for the most part, this is not yet the best way to acquire a healthy number of Bitcoins. The best way to acquire as much of this currency as you want right away is to purchase them with your traditional currencies.

These exchanges typically have a very basic and easy-to-understand system that allows you to effortlessly purchase your coins. You can also watch the markets through these exchanges to see how the currencies are doing and sell them. This is the very purpose of these systems, so there is not much more to them than that!

Choosing the Best Exchange for Your Needs

When it comes to choosing which cryptocurrency exchange will be best for you, there are a handful of things that you need to consider. Since these are completely digital and there is no form of governing body for cryptocurrencies, it is crucial that you are cautious and aware of what you are doing when you begin investing. You need to make sure that you are going with a reliable exchange that will work for your best benefit, as opposed to one that may be risky, shady or otherwise ineffective to deal with.

The following five criteria will be best for you to pay attention to when it comes to choosing a cryptocurrency exchange that works best for you. This will ensure that you choose one that will serve your needs and assist you in purchasing and selling your currencies and ultimately getting the most out of your Bitcoin experience.

Where Are You Located?

The first thing you need to consider is where you are located! Some exchanges deal exclusively with a single type of local currency. While there are always go-around ways to overcome these issues, ultimately you want to deal with an exchange that deals specifically with the country you are located in. This will help you bypass expensive fees, ensure you can access all of the features of the exchange, and will really help simplify the process overall. You want to keep this process as simple as possible to refrain from getting confused and making an accidental yet detrimental mistake that could cost you a large amount.

The best Bitcoin exchanges tend to be ones that are available in major countries. Many will deal with several countries so this will help ensure that you gain access to a well-known exchange which, as you will learn about, is highly recommended.

What Method of Payment Will You Use?

It is important that you look into what form of payment method you want to use when it comes to purchasing Bitcoins. Many exchanges only deal with certain forms of payments. This means that, to actually access the Bitcoins, you need to choose one that will support your chosen payment method.

One thing that is important to understand is that the easier it is for you to pay to purchase your Bitcoins the more fees you will pay for the service. While this is not always true, it is a general rule of thumb when it comes to exchanges. Still, many people believe that having that convenience makes paying the extra fees worthwhile as it makes acquiring their Bitcoins a lot easier.

What Are the Fees?

Now you need to think about the actual fees themselves! There are typically three types of fees that you will encounter on exchanges. These fees are the fees you pay to use the exchange services. They are somewhat like banking fees, only you get to choose how much you pay by choosing which service you will use. There are also ways of using exchanges, though it is not recommended, especially not for beginners.

So the first type of fee you will incur is called a Network Fee. This is a fee that you pay to the network or to the miners that ensures that your transaction will actually be processed. The standard fee for this is 0.00001 BTC, but it can vary. The faster your transactions are processed the more you can expect to pay for the service. Some exchange rates will have an automatic price set, whereas others may allow you to choose your price and, therefore, choose how quickly your transaction will be processed.

The next type of fee you will encounter is called a Conversion Fee. This is the fee that you pay to the exchange for converting your traditional currency to Bitcoin. This will be the same as paying a conversion fee to a bank for them exchanging your USD to CAD or through any similar type of conversion. Exchanges use this fee to make money so that they can keep their exchange running, and it typically is a very minimal fee. However, it is a good idea to take a look at the fee itself as it will vary between different exchanges.

The last type of fee you will incur is called a Maker and Taker Fee. These are the fees that you pay to the exchange for actually buying or selling your coins. They charge this as an opportunity to earn more profit once again. Typically, this profit is used to keep their systems running and their employees employed. This fee, once again, varies depending on which exchange you go to.

It is a good idea to look into the policies and fees of each exchange before you actually commit to one. Since they vary, you do not want to commit to one that may have astronomical fees in comparison to other exchanges. With no governing body, exchanges are essentially capable of determining their own chosen fees, and they can charge you anything they want. Of course, exchanges that charge unreasonably high fees and have poor services will not be considered credible, nor will their exchanges become popular. However, there are still many credible and popular services out there that charge fairly high rates. By paying attention to this, you can be clear as to what you are going into. You can also choose an exchange that will charge you the fairest fees in accordance with the services you are requesting from them.

Do They Deal with Bitcoin?

This may seem to be a fairly straightforward question, but you need to make sure that the exchange you are dealing with actually deals with Bitcoin. Since Bitcoin is the most popular form of cryptocurrency, the majority of credible exchanges do deal with it. For that reason, there may be two elements to look at here. First, obviously, you want to make sure they deal with Bitcoin. Second, however, is that you may want to consider what other coins you could potentially be interested in diversifying into in the future. If you do decide in the future that you want to invest in another form of cryptocurrency, choosing an exchange now that already deals with that currency can prevent you from having to relearn the systems and procedures on a new exchange once again. Finding a sort of "one-size-fits-all" exchange that will help you with all of the currencies you are interested in, as you become ready to invest, can ensure that you can keep everything simple. Don't forget, when it comes to investing in cryptocurrencies, simplicity is one of the key pieces of advice in preventing you from running into serious mistakes.

Is It Credible?

Lastly, you need to consider the credibility of the exchange. Typically, you want to look beyond reviews given on the exchange's website themselves. Instead, look toward actual reviews on the internet. Doing a simple search on the exchange name can help bring up reviews and information on past experiences that other users have had. There are many wonderful resources out there for determining how credible an exchange truly is and what you should look out for with certain exchanges. Finding one that is known to be secure, safe, time effective, and easy to use is best for beginners.

You can generally find this in larger-name exchanges. For that reason, it is typically better to stick to the ones that everyone is talking about. Then, not only can you ensure that they are most likely to be credible, but you can also find plenty of information on how they work and anything else you may need to know regarding the specific exchange you are considering working with!

The Buying Process

Now that you understand exchanges and how they work, as well as what to look for to find an exchange for you, it is time to understand the buying process! This will vary slightly from exchange to exchange, but, in general, it remains pretty well the same. There are a few steps, so make sure you pay attention to how this works.

Choose Your Exchange

You already know how to choose your exchange, but this *is* the first step. Choose one that you like, that makes sense to you, and that meets the criteria provided above. Then you can begin with the rest of the steps in the buying process.

Buy Bitcoins from the Exchange

When it comes to purchasing, each exchange will give you a set of guidelines to follow. For many, you can simply input your credit card or debit card information into the website and then purchase. The exchange will automatically deduct the chosen amount from your card and then provide you with your coins in exchange.

Some other forms of payments that are included in some exchanges include PayPal and bank check. Depending on where you are going and where the exchange is based, some will also let you pay in person.

After you have purchased your Bitcoin, they will appear in your wallet. You will learn more about wallets and the two types that you need to have in Chapter 4.

Transfer Bitcoins to a Wallet

Depending on the Bitcoin exchange, there are two things that will happen once you purchase your Bitcoins. You will either need to deposit them into your Bitcoin wallet that is separate from the exchange or, if it is an exchange like Coinbase, they will have a built-in hot wallet that you can use. Typically, the exchange will give you information on how you can deposit the coins into your wallet and what type of wallet is available to you.

The wallet that your coins are transferred into right away is known as a hot wallet. You want to transfer the coins to a cold wallet. Again, you will learn more about how this works in Chapter 4. However, it is important that you understand that this is a necessary step in the purchasing process as this is how you will protect your coins and prevent yourself from accidentally losing them or having them stolen from you.

Store or Spend Bitcoins

Once you have transferred your coins to your wallet, you can choose what to do. You can either store them long term in a cold wallet until you are ready to spend or sell them or you can keep them in a hot wallet to use for immediate spending or selling. You can also purchase what is now available as a "Bitcoin debit card", which acts just like a traditional debit card. This card keeps information about your current Bitcoin value and will allow you to spend them on any website or in any store that accepts Bitcoins as a form of payment.

Chapter 4: Storing Bitcoin

Now that you understand how Bitcoins are purchased, you need to understand how they are stored. This is absolutely necessary as the method through which you store your Bitcoins will ultimately result in them being protected or not. Proper storage will ensure that you can use them any time you need to but that they are not at risk of being lost or stolen. The way Bitcoins and other cryptocurrencies are stored is different from traditional currencies but also tends to be a lot more secure if you do it properly. If you will be investing in Bitcoin, it is essential that you learn to store them properly to protect your investment.

Types of Bitcoin Wallets

There are two types of Bitcoin wallets available to you when you begin purchasing and selling Bitcoin. They are hot wallets and cold wallets. Each wallet has a uniqueness to it based on the features, security level, and ease of access to the coins stored in that wallet.

The hot wallet is essentially the place where Bitcoins are immediately deposited upon purchasing or receiving them. This is a wallet where you can quickly and easily access your coins when you need or want them. This is a wallet that is connected to the internet and therefore can be tracked and accessed through the internet itself. Because it is plugged into the internet, this wallet tends to be less secure for long-term storage.

A cold wallet is a place where you can store your Bitcoins for the long haul. It is not connected to the internet and therefore anything stored in your cold wallet is safe from internet hackers. However, it is important that you also keep the information safe. Losing your cold wallet could result in you losing your Bitcoins forever.

To help you further understand how each wallet works and what you need to do to gain access to them, we will explore each one in detail. You should know that both forms of wallets are considered absolutely necessary if you will be investing in Bitcoin. Even though cold wallets may seem redundant and somewhat unnecessary, anyone investing any amount into Bitcoin should take advantage of these wallets and actually use them. They are the only way to completely protect yourself against hackers potentially stealing your funds.

Understanding and Using Hot Wallets

As I mentioned, hot wallets are the less secure form of wallet that is connected to the internet. The coins you store in here can be used right away as they are ready to be accessed by exchanges or sent to other Bitcoin wallets if you are purchasing something from someone or otherwise sending them money. These wallets are where your coins are initially deposited and where they can quickly be accessed.

To understand these wallets, consider them to be the same form of wallet as the one you carry in your pocket when you leave the house. This is where you store your funds that are available for immediate access. Just like with your physical wallet and traditional currency, you don't want to store any more funds in your hot wallet than you will actually need. This should be where the least amount of your funds is stored. You can store more here if you will be using them in the near future, such as if you are preparing to sell a large amount, but, otherwise, you do not want to keep your funds here in the long term.

The hot wallet that you use comes from one of two places: either built in to your exchange or hosted separately. Exchanges like Coinbase have built-in wallets that allow you to store and access your funds directly through the exchange. For people who are engaging in Bitcoin strictly for the purpose of trading them, this is a great way to access your coins quickly, trade them effortlessly, and ultimately keep them plugged into the exchange for quick sales.

For exchanges that don't have a built-in wallet, you will need to use one that is hosted separately. The most popular host for this type of wallet when it comes to Bitcoin is actually based on the Bitcoin website! This wallet can be "connected" to your exchange so that when you purchase Bitcoins, they can be deposited into it, but it is not hosted by the exchange. This type of hot wallet operates completely independently. For that reason, they typically have a wider range of what can be done with them and more customizability. While they are still just a space for you to store your coins and use them, they are not as restricted or bound by the rules of the exchange.

Making your hot wallet is simple: you either create an account with your Bitcoin exchange and the wallet is immediately formed or you go to a separate hot wallet hosting platform and create an account there. Once you do, you will be given personal "keys". These keys are encoded with information specific to your wallet. You should never share these keys as if anyone gets access to them they can hack into your wallet and steal your funds. Keep them completely private. You will also be given a set of public "keys", which is ultimately the information you would give to someone who wanted to send you some of the cryptocurrency.

Once you have deposited your newly purchased coins into this wallet, you can choose what to do. Again, you can either keep them in the hot wallet for quick access in regards to selling the coins, or purchasing products or services with them, or you can transfer them to a cold wallet for long-term storage. Doing that depends on the type of cold wallet you have chosen to use so you will find more information about the transferring process below.

Understanding and Using Cold Wallets

Cold wallets are a form of cryptocurrency wallet that is stored completely offline. The most popular form of cold wallet is a paper wallet. This is essentially a printed piece of paper with a special code on it that allows you to access your currencies when you want to. However, without the code, you cannot access them. This means that, since the code is not stored anywhere online, people are not capable of hacking into your wallet. It also means that you have to be very careful about the paper itself to prevent it from getting damaged or lost, which could result in your currency being lost as well.

Cold wallets are where investors store their cryptocurrencies long term. Here they are safe from theft. This means that you can move cryptocurrencies to your cold wallet and store them somewhere, such as a fireproof safe in your home, where they will remain until you choose to access them. Using this method is extremely safe. You can think of your cold wallet as your long-term savings account with your traditional bank. This account is one that cannot quickly be accessed, but it does keep your funds preserved until you are ready to access them. Then, since you are in control of it all, you can access them at any time by simply using the code on the paper.

The cold wallet keeps your private and public keys attached to it, but it also has a special code on it that links to the coins that have been moved to the offline space. This code is typically a QR code that can be scanned and put into your hot wallet to allow you to access these coins. It is important to understand that once you have scanned it and accessed the coins by the computer, they are now officially connected to the network. You will need to create a new cold wallet to place them back into the offline space and protect them once more.

Since the paper wallet is the most popular form of offline wallet, we will explore how you can make a paper wallet for your Bitcoins. However, if you are curious about other forms that exist, they include storing it on a hard drive or USB stick.

Now, to create your paper wallet, you will want to use the following steps:

1. Begin by opening your Bitcoin wallet. Log in and then access the Bitcoin paper wallet tool. This is available on the Bitcoin website itself, where the Bitcoin wallet is hosted.
2. Once you are there, save the page locally to your computer. The easiest way to do this is to tap "Ctrl-S" when you are on the page. Once you are done saving the page, you want to exit the page.
3. Shut down all of your internet pages. Then temporarily disconnect your computer from the internet. This will only be temporary, so don't worry about keeping it offline! You are not required to keep the computer offline forever to maintain the cold wallet.
4. Once your computer is completely disconnected from the internet, open the saved file on your desktop. While on the page, move the mouse around and type random characters into the text box as this creates "entropy", which is essentially

randomness. This makes it harder for anyone to hack into your cold wallet, in case it was ever compromised and exposed to the online space for some reason. This also assists you in creating your public and private key-pair for the cold wallet. Because this key-pair was created while you were disconnected from the internet, this is completely offline and therefore should not be accessible through the internet *unless* you connect your wallet to the internet once again. This is why you were to disconnect the internet in the first place.

5. Now, with your key-pair in order and your page set up, you need to print the page. Simply print it through your regular printer. If your printer is connected to the internet, be sure to disconnect it from the internet first and manually connect it to your computer. It is important that it is disconnected from the internet as well as your computer itself. This will ensure that

everything remains offline and safe!

6. The printed paper should feature two QR codes on it. One will say, "Public," and one will say, "Private." These are your wallet keys.
7. Now that your wallet is offline, you want to add funds to it! To do this, scan the public QR code attached to your wallet, and then send funds from your hot wallet to your cold wallet. This will be just like sending funds to any other standard Bitcoin transaction.
8. When you are ready to transfer all of your coins back to an online wallet, you will simply import the private key into any Bitcoin wallet online and conduct the transfer.

Note: Once you have done this, your private key will now be on the internet. While it is not available to anyone openly, hackers may now be able to access it. If you want to put funds back into a cold wallet, you will need to make a new cold wallet. Never reuse a cold wallet as once it has been connected it is compromised.

Note: If the paper with your keys on it becomes damaged or lost, there is no way to regain access to your funds. It is imperative that once you create your paper wallet or any other form of cold wallet, you are very careful as to where you place it. The best place is in a fireproof safe where no one aside from you has the information to get inside of the safe. Anywhere else may result in it becoming damaged or lost, which would result in you losing your investment.

Chapter 5: Trading Bitcoin

Buying Bitcoin is one part of the experience, but the part where everyone is currently making money is in trading it. Bitcoin has been the only cryptocurrency to rapidly grow and it continues to top the charts in regards to highest valued cryptocurrency available. If you really want to start earning some extra profits through this cryptocurrency, trading it is the best way to go.

In this chapter, we will explore the trading process itself. Please know that, while trading Bitcoin is the best way to make a profit, it is not always the best idea to sell *all* of your funds. With this coin regularly increasing in value, the best thing to do is to hold on to some of it and trade others. Stockpiling a set amount of Bitcoin is the best way to hedge yourself, but it also ensures that one day, when cryptocurrencies *do* become a regular-use currency, you already have some and are not left needing to purchase more!

Returning to the Cryptocurrency Exchange

Selling Bitcoins is essentially the opposite of buying Bitcoins. You will complete your selling process entirely through the same exchange where you purchased your coins, to begin with. On the majority of popular exchange websites, you gain access to systems that allow you to sell your stocks too!

Depending on what exchange you are using, the selling process should be simple. Major exchanges, such as Coinbase, simply have a page where you go in, type the amount that you want to sell, see how much your profit will be, and then sell it. This is not always instant as the exchange will need to match you up with a buyer who is prepared to purchase stocks. However, it is extremely simple. Some other exchanges may be a little more difficult so you will need to review the process itself on the page that you are on.

The standard process, however, is this: open your

exchange website, access the "selling" page, and key in how many Bitcoins you want to sell. Make sure your coins are available in your hot wallet so that they can easily be transferred into the exchange, and then hit "Go." Once you have, these coins are committed to the exchange and will be sold. You will then be returned with the value of your traditional currency based on what you sold your Bitcoins for.

What to Trade, What to Keep

How much of your Bitcoins you choose to trade and keep is ultimately up to you, though there are some general tips on what you should do to ensure that you maximize your profits. Which theory or practice you choose to follow will depend on why you got into cryptocurrencies in the first place. Are you preparing for the future or are you looking to earn profits?

If your primary concern is to prepare for the future, then it is important that you save a fair portion of the Bitcoins you have purchased and keep them aside in your cold wallet for as long as you can. People who got in for the purpose of preparing for what may be in store in our future in regards to cryptocurrencies typically keep anywhere from 40 to 80% of their coins in storage and never actually touch them. The other 20–60% are then traded actively on the market to earn a profit. This enables them to make more money now but also ensures that they have a fairly healthy stockpile set aside should cryptocurrency truly integrate into our society and become a commonly accepted form of currency.

If you are in it primarily for profit, the ratios at which you stockpile and trade will vary. Typically, you will want to trade between 40 and 80% of your Bitcoins and stockpile between 20 and 60%. This gives you the opportunity to keep a fairly healthy stockpile while also making a great profit so that you can enjoy your gains right away.

Where exactly you choose to sit on the scale of

how much you keep versus how much you actively trade will depend on two things: how much of your traditional cash you are willing to invest and how much of a risk you are willing to take. The more you keep, and the longer, the more you typically make. However, this could also result in you becoming exposed to various stock crashes where the profitability of the coin drops significantly. Trading in shorter time frames exposes you to a greater chance of positive profits but also means that you are less likely to gain as much. For this reason, some people actually split their investments *three* ways. One will be for stockpiling, and the rest is divided into long-term and short-term trades. This allows them to access almost-guaranteed profits right away while also holding out for the potential of the incredibly high profits that Bitcoin investors are famous for. It also allows them to store and hang on to an extra amount just in case we find ourselves in a Bitcoin-driven world where cryptocurrency is the new norm.

Again, how you choose to split yours depends on the risk you are willing to take, the reason you have gotten into Bitcoin in the first place, and what you are looking to gain from your investments. If you are completely unsure, start in a conservative investment style and work your way up from there until you find where you feel the most comfortable!

When to Pull the Trigger

Knowing when to pull the trigger is essential when it comes to investing. If you are purchasing Bitcoins with the intention of selling them later at a higher cost, you will need to know what to look for and when to sell. While this topic itself is one that may need an entire book of its own to explore in depth and with total thoroughness, there are many things that we can discuss right away to get you started.

First, the Bitcoin market is one that is best lived for long-term investments. Day trading is not ideal, as you are not likely to make any significant profit from this. You should plan to keep your investment in place for several weeks, or even months, if you are looking to do short-term investing. For long-term investing, you essentially want to leave it for as long as you can until you actually need the funds that you have invested *or* you see a good reason to withdraw, such as the market beginning to crash.

With traditional currencies, crashing markets are things we often come back from. For example, consider the recession of 2008. Although it has been a slow comeback, many people profited exponentially off of that because the comeback was virtually guaranteed. With Bitcoins and other cryptocurrencies, however, the guarantee is not so solid. While it typically comes back from dips, realistically the cryptocurrency market *could* completely collapse with no comeback if society were to decide it was not feasible and exit the market as a whole. While this is not expected to happen, it is a possibility. For that reason, you want to pay attention to the markets and, if necessary, sell. You can always re-enter the market when it stabilizes if it is just a temporary dip! That being said, don't sell every time the market takes a small turn. That would result in you selling constantly as the Bitcoin market, as with any market, fluctuates on a regular basis. As with regular stocks, the price is volatile and changes from day to day. The growth is typically seen over a long period of time as a steady incline overall.

So, all that being said, there are two times when you should sell your funds: you can sell your short-term funds at the start of a decline and then collect your profits and re-enter the market before the next incline if you want to gain profit quickly. Or you can simply leave your Bitcoins there to continue growing in profit and only withdraw from the market when you actually need the cash for something else. Otherwise, you should leave your coins in place, as they will continue to grow in value over time. The longer they are left alone the greater your profitability will become.

The best way to make sure that you pay attention to the market but don't give yourself anxiety over shifts in prices is to check in every few days. In the beginning, as you are getting used to the nature of the Bitcoin market pricing, you may desire to check once daily. However, reduce to checking in every other day or even every third day if you can. This will allow you to pay close attention and hopefully catch any potentially catastrophic drops before it's too late, but it also allows you to stay focused on your growth without becoming anxious from the constant rising and falling in prices.

Chapter 6: Mining Bitcoin

When the Bitcoin technology was launched, so was a unique opportunity: Bitcoin Mining. This is not anything like true mining, but it is something that is entirely necessary for the entire system to operate. These days, Bitcoin mining is a lot less lucrative than it once was. While it is still something you can earn a profit from, the profit has shrunk exponentially since the beginning. Furthermore, the more people that get involved in mining the less the profit there actually is. Still, it is good to understand what mining is. This will give you an idea of how it contributes to Bitcoin, the entire functionality of Bitcoin, and if there is any point in getting into mining these days!

What Is Mining?

Although mining is typically associated with the idea of digging for or "mining" products, Bitcoin mining does not operate like this. Instead, mining with Bitcoin actually refers to high-powered machines that are responsible for validating blocks of Bitcoin transactions. This results in these transactions being added to the blockchain. In return for their services, miners are rewarded with Bitcoins.

If Bitcoin mining did not exist, the entire concept of Bitcoin would not work. Mining, hashing transactions into blocks, and storing transactions on the blockchain are the three advancements that made Bitcoin the first cryptocurrency to actually work. These are responsible for not only processing transactions but also for doing it in a way that is highly secure and that protects all transactions from fraudulent activity.

Essentially, Bitcoin miners have equipped their high-power machines with software that actively solves complex math problems to verify transactions. As a result, they are rewarded Bitcoins in exchange for their services. This enables two things to happen: first, it is the entire system upon which Bitcoin was created. This is how they can produce secure transactions and protect Bitcoin users in a way that its attempted predecessors were unable to do. Second, it puts Bitcoins into circulation. Although the Bitcoins already exist, they are not in circulation until they have been awarded or "mined".

Through miners, the entire Bitcoin technology can run through what is known as a decentralized system. This was the revolutionary creation that made Bitcoin feasible: because there was no way to hack the system and produce fraudulent transactions. Since all nodes have to be in agreeance with one another to conduct a transaction, any transactions that are not considered valid are thus declined and therefore never put through to begin with.

How Does Mining Work?

The machines that miners use are typically built perfectly for the mining process. These are designed specifically for Bitcoin mining, therefore making them incredibly high-powered. Without these machines, you cannot engage in mining as you will not have enough power to support the process.

The machines that successfully complete the mining actions use what is called a SHA256 double round hash verification process. Through this process, the machines are able to validate the blocks of Bitcoin transactions. This validation process takes place before the transaction is then added to the blockchain itself. Once it has been added to the blockchain, the transaction cannot be reversed.

This is the process of validating transactions that ensures that they are secure and that they are not fraudulent. Any transaction that does not check out will be denied by the miner that is attempting to pass it, and therefore it will not make it to the blockchain. This means that the transaction will not be completed. When this happens, there is no way for anyone to know that the transaction was declined aside from the people attempting to conduct the transaction. The only permanent information about transactions is that which exists in the blockchain.

Mining is typically done by groups known as "mining pools". These mining pools are groups of individuals who join together and combine their power. This means that any blocks being mined are mined significantly faster and that they can verify far more blocks. As a result, they earn more. They then distribute their earnings around the pool in a predetermined way that enables everyone to earn some form of profit from the process.

Something worth understanding is that, no matter how powerful your mining pool or system is, you will not be able to exceed one block per ten minutes. This is the minimum amount of time required for new blocks to be added to the blockchain based on the algorithm, so it is impossible to exceed this rate. However, those who have high-powered machines and mining pools can typically reach this rate and are therefore mining at the fastest possible rate based on the algorithm and the power required to do so. If you are interested in understanding mining pools, we will discuss them further below.

Is Mining Still Profitable?

Bitcoin has a set number of coins that have been produced. The amount that already exists is the only amount that will ever exist. Unlike traditional currencies, there are no ways for anyone to increase the number of Bitcoins in existence. Not even the developers can produce more Bitcoins because they are based on a specific algorithm and, based on the requirement of the nodes to be in agreeance, it simply isn't possible.

However, not all of the Bitcoins are in circulation yet. This means that there is still the potential to make a profit. This does come with some risk though. In 2018, which is the time of this book being published, miners only make money if they are willing to spend a significant amount. Since there are already so many miners in existence and the supply of uncirculated Bitcoins is running out, it is much harder to gain a profit than it was in the beginning.

When it comes to understanding the profitability of Bitcoin mining, there are many things you need to consider. For starters, the cost of your electricity will increase significantly. To be able to host a machine that is powerful enough to mine Bitcoin, you will need a lot of power to actually power the machine. This means that you will be paying significantly more each month just to support the machine itself. This does not even factor in the cost of the machine, which varies in range. Some of them are less expensive but, remember, less expensive means less powerful and therefore less profit. In this day and age, power is everything.

Now, understanding the cost that goes into acquiring your hardware is something to consider. The biggest thing you must consider is the Hash Rate. This refers to how quickly your computer can solve the mathematical problems known as hashes. Ideally, to make a profit, you need a device that will have a very high hash rate, which will ensure that you can verify more blocks and therefore earn more profit.

Another thing to understand is that, if you get into mining, you have to join a mining pool. Mining on your own simply isn't profitable, and you won't be able to do much. So, it is a good idea to look at what mining pools are and the fees associated with them. We will discuss more about that in the following section. However, this does factor into the profitability of mining, so it is something to consider.

Bitcoins are built with an algorithm that automatically cuts the number of Bitcoins being issued in half every time a certain parameter is met. This means that, if you get started, you may be getting involved at a time when profitability is not high. Because there are already so many miners involved and many more joining all the time, this means that less profit is being rationed out over more people. As a result, it does significantly lower the profitability rate of mining.

Lastly, you have to consider the conversion rate. Since you are being paid in Bitcoins, you have to realize that, should the exchange rate ever decline, you may not get as much. So, say you are in the United States. If you get involved in mining, and the BTC to USD exchange drops, you will make significantly less profit. Since no one truly knows what will happen with Bitcoin, especially as we come closer to the end of new coins going into circulation, it is hard to predict how valuable Bitcoin will continue to be over time.

Understanding Mining Pools

Going to a mining pool is truly the only way to make any form of profit in this day and age. Mining pools, however, are something that you have to understand before you can become involved with them. A mining pool, as you now know, is a group of miners who get together and combine their mining power to mine more blocks. This means that the group is paid more. Because of how powerful these mining groups are, there is simply no way to compete with them on your own anymore.

Before you join a mining pool, it is essential that you research them. The best place to do that seems to be on the Bitcoin subreddit. This subreddit chain gives you plenty of information on various mining pools, including how their response is. The higher the mining pools response is the faster verifications are. As a result, the more money you make. However, having a high response rate also means that they have a large number of people in the group. A larger number of people means that the profits are being spread out more widely. So this would reduce your earnings ratio proportionately. Ideally, you would want to find a mining group that has a healthy response rate but not necessarily the highest one. This would signify that they are doing well and making a good profit and that they're not spreading it out over so many people. Finding that balance is essential in earning a profit.

The next thing you have to know is that every mining pool has fees. Typically, there is someone responsible for "administrating" the pool. As a result, you have to pay fees to the administrators to be a part of it. Every time you earn anything from the mining process, a small portion of that will be paid back to the mining pool in fees. Some mining pools have high fees, some have moderate and low fees. It is important that you completely understand these fees before you get involved. You should also take the time to understand any other policies or fees associated with the mining pool so that you are completely aware of what you are getting involved in once you join the pool. Each pool is operated and overlooked differently, so it is essential that you are clear on this and that you pay attention to these factors. This will ensure that you choose one that will maximize your profitability and be easy for you to be a part of, rather than one that will result in you not making as much income and potentially running into issues with the group.

Conclusion on Mining

Mining can still be profitable if you are willing to invest in the beginning. Having the best hardware that you can afford is absolutely necessary. The better your hardware the more likely you will be able to return a profit. You can determine how good the machine is based on its hash rate. The better the hash rate the more powerful the machine, and therefore the more profit you stand to make.

Before you begin investing in anything, though, you should consider how much power everything will take. You should also consider what the mining pool fees will cost and how much you will actually be paid out. There are many variables that go into mining, so unless you are willing to invest a fair number of funds and really give it your all, there will not be much profitability in this experience for you. If you are not prepared to invest in high-powered machinery and see the cost of your electricity go up, this may not be the route for you. However, if you are willing to invest in high-powered machinery and you find a mining pool that will work for you, mining is definitely still capable of being a profitable venture.

Chapter 7: The Future of Bitcoin

While the future is never guaranteed, there are many theories about what will happen with Bitcoin going forward. Since you are looking at investing, you are likely curious as to what the outlook for this currency is. This knowledge will give you an idea of whether or not it is worth it for you to get involved and will help you understand why people are so excited about this technology.

Remember that the theories given here are just that: theories. It is important to remain realistic on the fact that no one actually knows where Bitcoin and cryptocurrency itself are actually going in the future. While computer scientists are certainly working toward certain forms of reality, nothing is set in stone. The only true determining factor will be time itself. For that reason, it is a good idea to stay focused on the press and pay attention to cryptocurrency in the media. This will help you gain insight as to where we are at and where we are going. It will also give you some insight into any new developments or changes that may take place in the world of cryptocurrency.

Is It Here to Stay?

In short, yes. Whether anyone cares to admit it or not, Bitcoin is a powerful technology, and it is not going anywhere anytime soon. Although there is no way to predict the future, the history of Bitcoin has proven that it only gets stronger the more people disagree with it or question its fragility.

Cryptocurrency is something that has been in the making since the internet first gained popularity in the 1990s, and Bitcoin was the coin to finally produce results from those attempts. Based on how popular it has grown in the past decade, we can agree that Bitcoin is something many people are fascinated by and several people are "for".

Many people want to see a world where Bitcoin takes over and eliminates the need for currency exchanges, banks, and enormous banking fees. There are simply so many benefits to Bitcoin that everyone is eager to watch it succeed.

There is only one circumstance where we can predict that Bitcoin would fail, and that would be if someone came out with a better technology that would supersede what Bitcoin has already done. However, it is highly unlikely that this will happen. Although it is not impossible, far too many people have invested in Bitcoin and Bitcoin's growth to allow for it to simply fade away at this point. Thousands of miners and investors have all gotten on board, and it is highly unlikely that all of them will stray.

A lot of people believe that Bitcoin could have some form of major market crash once the entirety of the coin is in circulation. This may be true, but it is hard to say. Still, we are some ways away from that happening, so there is plenty of time to begin earning profits from Bitcoin.

The other thing that we need to consider is that Bitcoin is not the only cryptocurrency that is here to stay. Ethereum, Litecoin, and other cryptocurrencies that have since come out after the launch of Bitcoin are likely here to stay as well. Each form of cryptocurrency seems to have its own strengths and weaknesses that contribute to its place in the land of cryptocurrencies, so, at this point, none are expected to wipe out Bitcoin and take over as the apex cryptocurrency. Still, many are valid and worthwhile for investors in the long run.

Will It Always Be Bitcoin?

Bitcoin introduced a new form of protocol that had never existed prior to the launch of this cryptocurrency. We can pretty much guarantee that this protocol will continue to stick around and will serve in the cryptocurrency world for years to come. However, it is hard to say whether or not Bitcoin will always be "the one".

At this point, Bitcoin is the most widely accepted cryptocurrency. Because of its sheer popularity and value, more and more companies and individuals are accepting Bitcoin as a form of payment. It has already infiltrated the minds and wallets of many, meaning that the usage of it far exceeds most other cryptocurrencies. Even though others, such as Litecoin, seem to be easier to use for daily purchases, hardly anyone actually accepts these coins as a form of payment. The opposite can be said for Bitcoin.

That being said, right now, it is all about Bitcoin. It is hard to predict whether or not it will always be Bitcoin though. Realistically, a new coin could be introduced and could take over in the future, wiping out existing cryptocurrencies altogether and replacing them with a single currency that will do it all. If I'm being honest, that seems to be the future that many people are looking toward. However, just because a new and easier-to-use currency could become available it does not imply that Bitcoin itself would disappear. Bitcoin appears to be a "gold" of sorts in the cryptocurrency world.

Despite us not having any form of evidence or proof that Bitcoin will always be the apex cryptocurrency, it is still highly worthwhile to get involved in. If we were to wait on investing in things until they proved themselves one way or another in the future, we would never invest in anything. The earliest people to invest in Bitcoin had absolutely zero evidence that such a protocol would work, and yet now many of them are millionaires as a result of their investment. Bitcoin is currently the apex cryptocurrency and is continuing to make many people a fair amount of wealth. It is still an incredible cryptocurrency to get involved with in the present. The idea is not to avoid the currency altogether to see what happens but rather to pay attention and watch what is going on to ensure that you do not get burned through accidental ignorance. Paying close attention to the markets, as well as the rumors you hear in the news, is important. There is a saying in the investment and trading industries that says, "Act on the rumors, produce the news." This essentially means that when you hear that something will take place with Bitcoin, you act ahead of time, and then you are one of the ones in the news known for creating success instead of losing it all. By paying attention and making wise investment moves, you can make massive income with Bitcoin. It is certainly not an investment to be feared. It is simply one to pay attention to and watch out over as we continue to learn more about this cryptocurrency and all that it can do.

What Does the Prognosis for Cryptocurrency Evolution Look Like?

Since the launch of cryptocurrencies, the prognosis for cryptocurrency evolution has been considered by many. Everyone is curious about what Bitcoin means, and what we will do with it. To give you an idea of what an ideal future with

Bitcoin fully integrated would look like, let's take a look at what the common consensus is when we consider a world with Bitcoin, or any major cryptocurrency, as the primary currency.

Faster, Cost-Effective Bank Transfers

At this time, banks are the only way for us to conduct any form of financial interactions. This means that we are forced to pay massive fees for a variety of services. For example, transferring funds from one bank to another can cost a great deal! Additionally, many banks charge monthly fees for using their services that cut into our profits as well. When you factor in the potential of overseas transfers, the entire cost drives up even more. Bitcoin completely eliminates all of these fees.

While Bitcoin does come with many fees, such as those you pay to the exchanges and those you pay for transactions, there is a lot more freedom in the fees you pay. Since you are in charge and you are privately responsible for your funds, you get to choose which exchanges to use and which fees you want to pay for transactions. As a result, you can choose to pay virtually nothing per transaction or pay more to increase the speed of your transaction. This gives you more power to determine how much your banking actually costs and can enable you to save massive amounts of money.

Increase in Global Remittances

To date, members of first-world countries are responsible for sending more than $500 billion in remittances to third-world and developing countries. This far exceeds the amount of money governments send to these countries, which is vital for their growth and development. Since these people are all using banks, they are also paying fees that typically range anywhere from 6 to 10%. This is a lot of money that goes toward fees rather than into the pockets of those in these third-world and developing countries!

If these people had access to a global currency that was not subjected to banking fees and conversion fees, far more money would land in the pockets of those being sent the money instead of in the pockets of the banks. This could mean incredible things for individuals in these developing countries who are desperately in need of the funds.

Safe Money for Developing Countries

In developing countries, robbery is a major issue. Since there are few places where wealth can be stored in these countries, it is easy for robbers to come in and take everything a person has. If they were to conduct everything through cryptocurrencies, however, their funds would be stored entirely online, protected by private keys. This means that there would be no potential for robbers to easily come in and wipe a person out. This would also protect them against the high fees that their banks charge, sometimes reaching as high as 20% or more!

In addition to reducing the risk of robbery and minimizing fees, having access to a cryptocurrency in a country such as Africa would result in people being protected against high-inflation risks. At this time, these individuals are regularly exposed to the risk of their currency becoming worth less and less while the value of products goes up significantly. This means they are at a major disadvantage in being unable to afford the necessities that are required for them and their families to live. If they had access to a cryptocurrency that was accepted across the globe, there would be no way for their currency to deflate in price or the cost of goods and services to inflate beyond the rate of what their cash is worth. They would be given an equal opportunity to have a valuable form of currency, giving them a better chance at being able to afford the necessities associated with living.

Increased E-Commerce Benefits

Bitcoin is a digital-based currency, so, naturally, it comes with many benefits for people in the e-commerce space. Specifically, Bitcoin gives people the opportunity to conduct international business while paying significantly fewer expenses. The amount it would cost for a shop to conduct business overseas, either purchasing or shipping, would be far more attainable than it currently is. Since there would be no currency exchange fees, banking fees or otherwise, they would be able to retain a higher amount of profit and therefore experience greater success.

It also allows consumers to engage in business overseas too. Since the risk of fraudulent activity is minimized, they become far more likely to want to purchase things from e-commerce stores in countries that are currently considered "risky" based on fraudulent experiences.

Empowers the Public

For the past several decades, we have been forced to entrust banks with our funds. Because of the way payrolls and bills are currently paid, we cannot choose to be bank-free because then we cannot get paid and pay our bills. There is really no way around the banking system, meaning we have no choice but to take part in it. If you do not have a bank account, you cannot establish credit, and therefore you cannot even get the electricity turned on at your house in most places. This means we are literally forced into the banking system, with no alternatives or choices.

If cryptocurrency came into the foreground and trumped traditional currencies, the public would be given alternatives to the traditional banking institutions. We would be able to determine who we want to entrust our funds with, how, and what policies and philosophies we have around our funds. We would be able to then choose exchanges, wallets, and other financial services that adequately align with our needs, rather than be forced into ones that may or may not actually align with us.

We would be able to directly pay for things and perform transactions free of the banks, and the services would ideally become more efficient and user-friendly. As a result, we would truly have more power and say in how our finances are managed and used. It would keep a lot more in our pockets, and a lot less would be thrown into various fees and expenses that we are presently forced to pay just to partake in society.

Conclusion

Cryptocurrencies have been idealized since the mid-1990s but were not "conquered" until 2009. When Satoshi Nakamoto introduced Bitcoin in 2009, the world as we know it changed. This was the first *ever* of its kind to officially exist in a way that made cryptocurrency secure, accessible, and usable. Ever since its launch, Bitcoin has grown in popularity and in value.

These days, Bitcoin has evolved from being a hot topic for investors and computer scientists to being a hot topic for just about everyone. Everyone is wondering how they can get involved in investing in this form of currency, what is necessary to get started, and how they can begin earning profits from Bitcoin. Luckily, you now have all of the information you need to get started!

I hope that by reading this guide you were able to understand everything about Bitcoin and why it is such a revolutionary and fascinating currency.

I hope you are also able to now begin investing in the currency and getting your desired results from it. Whether you want to stockpile it for the future that is inevitably coming or trade it to earn a profit now, you officially have all of the information you need to get started.

The next step is to return back to Chapter 3: "Buying Bitcoin" and begin the buying process! Find yourself a reliable exchange, purchase your coins, and then store them safely as you were taught in Chapter 4: "Storing Bitcoin." From there, you can do anything you feel is right with your coins. Whether you want to hold on to them for long-term growth, trade them in the short term or simply stockpile them, you should now have all the information you need to do just that.

Lastly, if you enjoyed this book, I ask that you please take the time to honestly review it on Amazon Kindle. Your feedback would be greatly appreciated.

Thank you.

www.ingramcontent.com/pod-product-compliance
Lightning Source LLC
Chambersburg PA
CBHW030444220526
45464CB00006B/2416